MORE

CRACK YOURSELF ≈UP≈ JOKES FOR KIDS

Other books by Sandy Silverthorne

MORE
CRACK YOURSELF UP
JOKES FOR KIDS

SANDY SILVERTHORNE

SPIRE

Published by Revell
a division of Baker Publishing Group
PO Box 6287, Grand Rapids, MI 49516-6287
www.revellbooks.com

Printed in the United States of America

Library of Congress Cataloging-in-Publication Data
Names: Silverthorne, Sandy, 1951– author.
Title: More crack yourself up jokes for kids / Sandy Silverthorne.
Description: Grand Rapids : Revell, 2019.
Identifiers: LCCN 2018045198 | ISBN 9780800729707 (pbk. : alk. paper)
Subjects: LCSH: Wit and humor, Juvenile.
Classification: LCC PN6166 .S57 2019 | DDC 818/.602—dc23
LC record available at https://lccn.loc.gov/2018045198

Author is represented by WordServe Literary Group (www.wordserveliterary.com).

19 20 21 22 23 24 25   7 6 5 4 3 2 1

To Vicki, my wife, my love, and my best friend:
You are truly a gift from the Lord. If it weren't for you,
I wouldn't be doing any of this. Thanks for letting me
crack myself up again.

To Christy: I learn from you every day. And not just
computer stuff either. I love your commitment
to loving Jesus and other people. And together,
we're joke makers.

To Lonnie at Baker Publishing Group and Nick at
WordServe Literary: Big thanks for making this book
happen. You're the best!

You've cracked yourself up with the first joke book; now are you ready for some more? More giggles, more chuckles, more laughs? Do you want to make your friends, your family, and even your teachers crack up a little *more*?

This book has *more* one-liners, *more* knock-knock jokes, *more* puns, *more* riddles, and even *more* hilarious illustrations. Throw in some truly impossible tongue twisters, and this is the book for you! So what are you waiting for? Get ready to read and laugh and giggle and crack yourself up even *more*!

Q: How does the Man in the Moon give himself a haircut?

A: Eclipse it.

Q: What did the mom broom say to the baby broom?

A: "Time to go to sweep, dear."

Q: What has four wheels and gives milk?

A: A cow on a skateboard.

Q: Why is a bee's hair always sticky?

A: Because they use honeycombs!

Q: Why did the man keep running around his bed?

A: Because he was trying to catch up on his sleep!

Caden: Will this road take me to Springfield?
Max: Nope. You're going to have to drive yourself.

Lonny: What's a runner's favorite subject in school?
Donny: Jog-raphy.

Christy: What is a kitten's favorite movie?

Misty: *The Sound of Mewsic.*

Q: What did the book name his daughter?

A: Page.

Q: What has four legs and flies?

A: Two birds.

Q: You break it every time you say it. What is it?

A: Silence.

Q: Where do whales go to hear music?

A: To the orca-stra!

Okay, once more from the top.

Q: Where do sheep go on vacation?

A: To the Baa-hamas.

Joe: What has four eyes but can't see?
Bo: Mississippi.

Jon: What can you catch but can't ever throw?
Ron: A cold.

Dan: What do you call a cow who cuts your grass?
Jan: A lawn mooer.

Brian: Where's a good place to store your dog?
Ryan: In the barking lot.

Patient: Doctor, I have a ringing in my ears. What should I do?

Doctor: Get an unlisted number.

Q: What's a dog's favorite breakfast?

A: Pooched eggs.

Two eggs Rover easy.

Peg: What is salty and delicious and flies to the moon?

Meg: A rocket chip!

Q: What do fish take to stay healthy?

A: Vitamin Sea.

Max: What do you call a dog who loves having its hair washed?

Alsea: A shampoodle.

Q: What's black and white, black and white, black and white and green?

A: Three skunks fighting over a pickle.

Chad: What's a dog's favorite kind of pizza?
Rad: Pupperoni.

Ed: What do military camels wear?
Ned: Camelflage.

Rowan: How many sheep do you need to make a sweater?
Remy: I don't know; none of my sheep can knit.

Ava: What creature is smarter than a talking parrot?
Isabelle: A spelling bee!

Knock, knock.
Who's there?
Oliver.
Oliver who?
Oliver sudden I don't feel so good.

Teacher: Alex, which months have 28 days?
Alex: All of them!

Braeden: What is a lumberjack's favorite month?
Caden: Septimmmberrr!

Fred: Where does an astronaut park the space shuttle?

Charlotte: At a parking meteor.

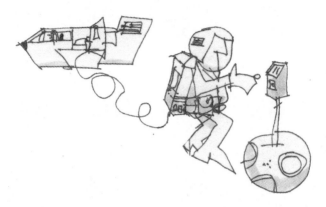

Q: What do a tomato and a bicycle have in common?

A: They both have handlebars. Except the tomato.

Q: What should you do when a bull charges you?

A: Pay him.

Q: What starts with *t*, ends with *t*, and is full of *t*?

A: A teapot.

Teacher: How many seconds are there in a year?

Smart Aleck: Twelve. January 2nd, February 2nd, March 2nd . . .

Q: What does a gorilla use to fix the sink?

A: A monkey wrench.

Q: What can you have in your pocket while your pocket's still empty?

A: A hole.

I stayed in a really old hotel last night. They sent me a wake-up letter.

The Time Traveler is
here to see you.

Tell him to come back
yesterday.

Len: How did the giraffe do in his classes?
Ben: He got high honors.

Jack: What did the sun say to Mercury?
Zach: "Can you give me some space?"

Q: What's the only grade you can plant a flower in?

A: Kindergarden!

Q: **What starts with *p* and ends with *e* and has a thousand letters?**

A: Post office.

Q: **A man arrives in a small town on Friday. He stays three days, then leaves on Friday. How is this possible?**

A: Friday is the name of his horse.

Q: **What belongs to you but others use it much more than you?**

A: Your name.

Q: **David's father has three sons: Snap, Crackle, and _____?**

A: No, silly. David!

Tongue Twisters

A synonym for cinnamon is a cinnamon synonym.

The great Greek grape growers grow great Greek grapes.

Any noise annoys an oyster, but a noisy noise annoys an oyster more.

Growing gray goats graze great green grassy groves.

Sal: Did you hear about the amazing invention that allows people to see through walls?

Hal: What is it?

Sal: A window.

Q: What is brown and has a head and a tail but no legs?

A: A penny.

Q: Why did the cow cross the road?

A: It was going to the moo-vies.

Q: Where do frogs fly their flags?

A: Up tadpoles.

Mason: What did you find when you traced your family tree?

Jason: Termites.

Teacher: James, why is your homework in your father's handwriting?

James: I used his pen!

Teacher: Joey, could you please pay a little attention?

Joey: I'm paying as little as I can.

Teacher: Why are you so late this morning?

Whitney: The sign said, "School Ahead, Go Slow."

Ron: Why did the musician put his guitar in the refrigerator?

Jon: He wanted to play some cool music.

Teacher: Now, kids, when I ask this next question, I want you to answer at once. What is three plus two?

Class: At once!

Q: Why did the painting go to prison?

A: Because it was framed.

Q: What happens when a policeman goes to bed?

A: He becomes an undercover cop.

Q: Where do bulls put their messages?

A: On the bull-etin board.

Q: What do you get when you cross a jet with a hamburger?

A: Some very fast food.

Hal: What are the biggest ants in the world?
Sal: Eleph-ants.

Q: Why do hummingbirds hum?
A: They forgot the words!

Chloe: My aunt lost 10 pounds on her trip to London.
Kylie: Wow, how did she do that?
Chloe: She left her wallet on a bus.

Q: What did one pencil say to the other pencil?
A: "You're looking sharp."

Q: What did one genius say to the other genius?

A: "You're looking smart."

Q: What did one puzzle say to the other puzzle?

A: "You look put together."

Q: What did one dog say to the other dog?

A: "You look fetching."

Sandy: What did the beach say to the tide as it came in?

Sunny: "Long time, no sea."

Q: What did one track runner say to the other track runner?

A: "You look dashing."

Q: What did the bacon say to the tomato?

A: "Lettuce get together."

Jason: Why did the gardener plant money in the ground?

Mason: He wanted his soil to be rich.

Jen: Why did the robber take a bath?

Ben: He wanted to make a clean getaway.

Ben: What do you get when you cross a fish and an elephant?

Len: Swimming trunks.

Q: What kind of beans do llamas like?

A: Llama beans, naturally.

Randy: What do you call a chicken who wakes you up in the morning?

Andy: An alarm cluck.

Logan: What do you say when you lose a Wii game?

Rogan: "I want a Wii-match!"

Q: Why did the golfer wear two pairs of pants?

A: In case he got a hole in one.

Donny: Why did the guy put a clock under his desk?

Lonny: Because he wanted to work overtime.

Q: What do you get when you cross a cow and a duck?

A: Milk and quackers.

Q: What runs but never gets anywhere?

A: A refrigerator.

Q: What do you get when you cross a cat with a lemon?

A: A sour puss.

Q: Where do sheep go to get their hair cut?

A: To the baa-baa shop.

Q: Why did the M&M go to college?

A: He wanted to be a Smartie.

Q: Why did the tree go to the dentist?

A: It needed a root canal.

Q: What is one word that looks the same upside down?

A: SWIMS.

Patient: Doctor, I'm convinced I'm a pretzel.
Doctor: Don't worry. I'll straighten you out in no time.

Stan: Did you hear the story about the broken pencil?
Dan: No.
Stan: Never mind. It's kind of pointless.

Ed: Why did the kid bring string to the soccer game?

Ted: He wanted to tie the score.

Macy: Did you hear about the pet store owner who couldn't sell his porcupine?

Lacy: Yeah, he was stuck with it.

Don: Do you know why the guy was fired from the calendar factory?

Ron: He took a day off.

Q: What goes into the water green and comes out blue?

A: A frog on a cold day.

Harper: What's brown, has antlers, and squeaks?

Asher: A moose on a rusty bike.

Q: What do you drop when you need it but take back when you don't?

A: An anchor.

Knock, knock.
Who's there?
Etch.
Etch who?
Gesundheit.

Q: What three letters can frighten a burglar?
A: ICU.

Stan: Did I tell you the construction joke?
Dan: Nope.
Stan: I'm still working on it.

Q: Why did the cow cross the road?

A: To get to the udder side.

Q: What pet makes the loudest noise?

A: A trum-pet.

I couldn't remember how to throw a boomerang. But eventually it came back to me.

I was going to look for my missing watch but I never could find the time.

Q: What does a thesaurus eat for breakfast?

A: A synonym roll.

Jon: How does a dog stop a DVD?
Ron: He hits the paws button.

Bo: How does a mouse feel after a shower?
Jo: Squeaky clean.

Terry: What do you call an elephant in a phone booth?

Mary: Stuck!

Q: What do giant whales eat?

A: Fish and ships.

Q: What do you give a pig with poison oak?

A: Oinkment.

Q: What's a frog's favorite drink?

A: Croaka-Cola.

Q: Who makes dinosaur clothes?

A: A dino-sewer.

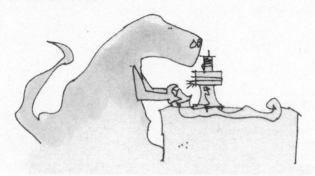

Knock, knock.

Who's there?

Luke.

Luke who?

Luke through the peephole and see for yourself.

Alsea: Where do hamburgers go to dance?

Max: The meat ball.

Warden: How would you like to celebrate your birthday?

Inmate: What would you think of an open house?

Q: What dinosaur loves to sleep?

A: A Stego-snore-us.

Sam: What do Santa's helpers learn at school?

Pam: The elf-abet.

Q: What kind of lion never roars?

A: A dande-lion.

Q: What runs around a yard but never moves?

A: A fence.

Q: What do you call a bear that flies and never grows up?

A: Peter Panda.

Q: What's an Australian bear's favorite soft drink?

A: Coca-Koala.

Q: How do you know if there's an elephant under your bed?

A: Your head hits the ceiling.

Q: Why did the elephant paint himself lots of colors?

A: So he could hide in the crayon box.

Q: How can you tell if an elephant has been in your refrigerator?

A: From the footprints in the butter.

Q: How can you tell if an elephant has been in your pantry?

A: The peanuts are all gone.

Tongue Twisters

Which Swiss wristwatches are the real Swiss wristwatches?

Cooks cook cupcakes quickly.

Does your sport shop stock short socks with spots?

Chop shops stock chops.

Imagine an imaginary menagerie manager.

Q: What's gray and goes round and round?

A: An elephant in a dryer.

Q: Why did the elephant float down the river on his back?

A: So he wouldn't get his tennis shoes wet.

Q: Why do elephants wear sandals?

A: So they won't sink in the sand.

Q: Why do ostriches stick their heads in the ground?

A: They're looking for elephants who forgot to wear their sandals.

Hannah: What has four legs, a trunk, and sunglasses?

Deagan: A mouse on vacation.

Q: Where do people go when they have two broken legs?

A: Nowhere.

Donny: What's worse than raining cats and dogs?

Lonny: Hailing taxi cabs.

Max: How do kittens shop?
Jax: They order from cat-alogs.

Q: What do you call it when you paint a picture of your cat's feet?

A: A paw-trait.

Q: What do you call a confused cat?

A: Purr-plexed.

Q: What's a cat's favorite color?

A: Purr-ple.

Q: What's a snake's favorite subject in school?

A: Hissstory.

Ted: What did the teddy bear say after dinner?
Ned: "I'm stuffed!"

The optimist says the glass is half full. The pessimist says the glass is half empty. The mother says, "Why didn't you use a coaster?"

Farmer Brown: What did the mom cow say to the baby cow?

Mrs. Brown: "It's pasture bedtime."

Q: What's a cow's favorite holiday?

A: Moo Year's Day.

Q: What do you call a stampede at a cow ranch?

A: Udder chaos.

    Bob: Why did the Secret Service surround the president with cows?

    Rob: Because they wanted to beef up security.

Q: What's a cow's favorite type of math?

A: Cow-culus.

Q: What do you get when you cross an angry cow with an annoyed sheep?

A: An animal that's in a baaad mooood.

Q: What's the difference between a dog and a marine biologist?

A: One wags a tail, and the other tags a whale.

Ron: Why did the giant wear a baseball glove?
Jon: He was hoping to catch a bus.

Mason: What's a dog's favorite profession?
Jason: Bark-eology.

Q: Where do the cows eat lunch?

A: In the calf-eteria.

Q: What two things can you never eat for breakfast?

A: Lunch and dinner.

Q: What's gray and beautiful and wears a glass slipper?

A: Cinderella-phant.

Q: What do you get when you cross a Labrador, a poodle, and a magician?

A: A Labracadabradoodle.

Iris: Twenty kids tried to get under one umbrella and, believe it or not, none of them got wet.

Bo: How did that happen?

Iris: It wasn't raining.

Q: What do you call two guys hanging on a window?

A: Kurt and Rod.

Q: What's a bunny's favorite music?

A: Hip-hop.

Tim: Why did the guy get fired from the orange juice factory?

Kim: He couldn't concentrate.

Teacher: Sandy, use the word *rhythm* in a sentence.

Sandy: My brother is going to the movies, and I want to go rhythm.

Aiden: Dad, I've got great news. Remember when you said you'd give me $500 if I got good grades this term?

Dad: Yeah. Sure.

Aiden: Well, you get to keep the money!

Mom, what's it like to have the best daughter in the whole world?

I don't know, dear. You'll have to ask Grandma.

Q: What bug arrests all the other bugs?
A: A cop-roach.

Q: What candy do you eat on the playground?
A: Recess Pieces.

Bill: Why couldn't the cookie reach the table?
Phil: Because it was a shortbread.

Knock, knock.
Who's there?
Abbott.
Abbott who?
Abbott you don't know who this is.

Harper: Have you ever seen a catfish?
Asher: No, how does he hold the fishing pole?

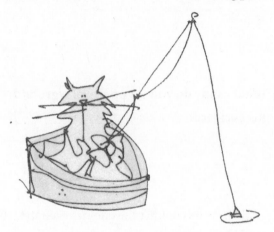

Q: What kind of keys do kids like to carry?

A: Cookies!

Q: Where did the kittens go on their school field trip?

A: To the mewseum.

Q: How do bees get to school?

A: On the school buzz of course.

Bill: What happens when it rains cats and dogs?

Jill: You might step in a poodle.

Q: Why did the police hire the duck?

A: They wanted him to quack the case.

Terry: Why did the teacher bring crackers to school?

Jerry: It was parrot-teacher conference day.

Max: Why did the elephant sit on the marshmallow?

Alsea: He didn't want to fall in the hot chocolate.

Q: When does a horse talk?

A: Whinny wants to.

Q: How do bunnies travel?

A: By hareplane.

Q: What do you call a bunch of smart trees?

A: A brainforest.

Q: What do you call a guy who owns a truck?

A: Van.

Q: What do you get when you cross a dinosaur with a pig?

A: Jurassic Pork.

Sage Advice: Never argue with a fool; he may be doing the same thing.

Q: What is a pirate's favorite tool?

A: A sea saw.

Q: Why are some fish at the bottom of the ocean?

A: They dropped out of school.

Q: Where is a car most likely to get a flat tire?

A: At a fork in the road.

Mason: Why did the baby strawberry cry?
Jason: Because his folks were in a jam.

Q: What's a gymnast's favorite season?

A: Spring.

Q: How is a baseball team similar to a muffin?

A: They both depend on the batter.

Q: What do firefighters put in their soup?

A: Firecrackers.

Q: Why was the broom late for class?

A: It overswept.

Bo: Why did the girl bring lipstick and eye shadow to class?

Iris: She had a makeup exam.

When I see a cookie, I hear two voices in my head. One says, "You need to eat that cookie." The other one says, "You heard him, eat that cookie."

Bus Driver (to passenger): Don't you want to take a seat?

Passenger: No thanks. I already have enough to carry.

Misty: What's the name of your new dog?

Christy: I don't know; he won't tell me.

Q: Why didn't the hatchet go to the party?

A: It wasn't axed.

Caden: Do you know how to keep a dummy in suspense?

Braeden: No, how?

Caden: I'll tell you tomorrow.

Teacher: Carlos, go to the map and point to North America.

Carlos: (*Points to the map.*) Here it is.

Teacher: Good job! Now, class, who discovered North America?

Class: Carlos!

Ted: Where do you put smart hot dogs?

Ned: On honor rolls!

Q: What do you call a funny chicken?

A: A comedi-hen.

Wife: Doctor, you've got to help us. For five years, my husband has been convinced he's a chicken.

Doctor: Why didn't you call me earlier?

Wife: We needed the eggs.

Q: What's red and orange and knocks you over?

A: Tackle Me Elmo.

Q: Where do crayons go on vacation?

A: Color-ado!

Jan: Why did the boy take a pencil to his bedroom?

Dan: He wanted to draw the curtains.

I'm a little nervous. This is my first operation.
Don't worry. It's mine too.

Asher: What do you call it when you have Grandma on speed dial?

Bo: Insta-Gram.

Q: What do you call a bee who's having a bad hair day?

A: A Frizzbee.

Did you hear about the paddle sale at the boat store?
  It was quite an oar-deal.

Did you hear about the limo driver who didn't have a customer for 25 years?
  He worked all that time and had nothing to chauffer it.

Tongue Twisters

A box of mixed biscuits, a mixed biscuit box.

The sixth sick sheik's sixth sick sheep.

What time does the wristwatch strap shop shut?

Flash message! Flash message!

Six thick sticky thistle sticks.

Why do you drive on a parkway but park on a driveway?

Knock, knock.
Who's there?
Scott.
Scott who?
Scott nothing to do with you.

Q: Why can you never go hungry at the beach?

A: You can always eat the sand which is there.

Q: What do pigs use to write a letter?

A: A pigpen.

Teacher: Rylie, which hand do you like to write with?

Rylie: Neither. I like to use a pencil.

Q: What did one rubber band say to the other rubber band?

A: "Snap out of it!"

Hal: What do you give a baker's daughter on your first date?
Sal: Flours.

Q: What did the police officer say to his sweater?

A: "Do you know why I pulled you over?"

Q: Why did the baker work overtime?

A: He kneaded the dough.

Q: Why did the belt get arrested?

A: Because it held up a pair of pants.

Donny: Where do birds invest their money?
Lonny: In the stork market.

Q: What are caterpillars afraid of?

A: Dogger-pillars.

Q: What do you call a bear who's caught in the rain?

A: A drizzly bear.

Dad: What did you learn in school today?

Kid: They taught us how to write.

Dad: Wow, what did you write?

Kid: I don't know; they haven't taught us how to read yet.

Q: What did the baby corn say to the mama corn?

A: "Where's Pop?"

I used to be indecisive. Now I'm not so sure.

Sam: Dad, I got a *D* in math.
Dad: Well, what are we going to do?
Sam: For one thing, I need you to stop doing my homework.

Ditzy Girl: My father flew in for the weekend.
Friend: Oh, how nice. Did you meet him at the airport?
Ditzy Girl: Oh no, I've known him all my life.

Q: What do you call a web page for an optometrist?

A: A site for sore eyes.

Husband: Happy Birthday! Remember that bright red Porsche you've always wanted?

Wife: Why yes, dear.

Husband: Good, 'cause I got you a toothbrush in the exact same color!

Teacher: Be sure you go straight home.

Boy: I can't. I live around the corner.

Q: What did the big bucket say to the small bucket?

A: "You look a little pail."

Q: Where do horses go shopping?

A: Old Neighvy.

I got fired from my job in the kitchen for stealing utensils. It was a whisk I was willing to take.

Terry: Why did the policeman bring a jar of peanut butter to the freeway?

Jerry: He heard there was a traffic jam.

Q: What do you get when you cross a rabbit with a frog?

A: A bunny ribbit.

Did you hear about the postal worker who was upset?
   He got mad and stamped his feet.

Rod: Why is tennis such a loud game?
Todd: Because all the players raise a racket.

Q: What's the world's largest punctuation mark?
A: The 100-yard dash.

Mason: What do you call a dinosaur who's at the bottom of the sea?

Jason: A Tyrannosaurus Wreck.

Q: What's the tallest piece of furniture?

A: A bookcase. It's got the most stories.

Q: What do you get when you cross a carrier pigeon with a parrot?

A: A carrier pigeon who stops to ask for directions.

So you go down two blocks, past the delicatessen, then turn left...

Movie Ticket Seller: I'm sorry. We're all sold out—
right down to the last seat.

Customer: Great! I'll take the last seat,
please.

Q: Why did the chicken cross the playground?
A: To get to the other slide.

Randy: I've forgotten everything I've ever
learned.
Andy: Well, what do you know!

Q: What's yellow and goes "Ho, ho, ho"?
A: Santa Banana.

Bill: Somebody robbed the bakery yesterday.
Jill: Well, doesn't that take the cake!

Ron: Why did Alice wear only one boot?
Jon: She heard the snow was one foot deep.

Max: What's worse than being with a fool?
Jax: Fooling with a bee.

Knew a lady who loved a bargain. She bought everything that was marked down. Last week she brought home an elevator.

Mason: Where do sharks go on vacation?
Jason: Finland.

Teacher: Joey, where can you find the Red Sea?
Joey: Usually on my report card.

Scientist 1: I see your microscope magnifies three times.
Scientist 2: Oh rats! I've used it twice already!

City Guy: How do you stop moles from digging in your garden?
Farmer: Easy. Hide the shovel.

Judge: You have a choice: 30 days in jail or $100.
Convict: I'll take the money!

Sue: Why does Philip jump up and down before drinking his chocolate milk?
Fred: Because the carton says, "Shake well before using."

Q: What did the nut say when it sneezed?

A: "Cashew!"

Q: Why won't the shrimp share his lunch?

A: 'Cause he's a little shellfish.

Q: What's a small dog's favorite soft drink?

A: Pupsi-Cola.

Q: What is flat and golden brown and doesn't want to grow up?

A: Peter Pancake.

Kid: I can't figure out this math problem.

Teacher: Are you serious? Any five-year-old can figure that out!

Kid: Well, no wonder. I'm eight.

Q: Where do sea otters keep their space station?

A: In otter space.

Have you heard about the new movie about a fruit farmer?
It's rated Peachy-13.

Q: What's big and gray and has horns?

A: An elephant marching band.

Doctor: What seems to be the trouble?
Patient: I keep thinking that no one can hear me.
Doctor: What seems to be the trouble?

Q: What do you get when you cross a small bear with a skunk?

A: Winnie the Pew.

Q: Where do ducks look up words?

A: In the duck-tionary.

Ron: How can you tell if there's an elephant in your peanut butter?

Don: Check the list of ingredients.

Q: Where do mice go while wearing costumes?

A: A mousequerade party.

Q: What's a hog's favorite game?

A: Pig-pong.

Patient: Doctor, I'm convinced I'm a needle and thread!

Doctor: How do you feel?

Patient: Sew-sew.

Man: Doctor, I think I'm a parachute!

Doctor: Call me next week when I have an opening.

Q: What has 100 feet and says, "Ho, ho, ho"?

A: A Santa-pede.

Man: Doctor, I'm convinced I'm a smoke detector.

Doctor: Don't worry. There's no cause for alarm.

Q: What's a pig's favorite winter Olympic sport?

A: Ice hoggy.

Hans: Where do old Vikings live?
Swen: In Norse-ing homes.

Patient: Doctor, I'm convinced I'm an umbrella!
Doctor: Oh, you must be under the weather.

Man: Doctor, I'm convinced I'm a bridge!
Doctor: Oh my, what's come over you?
Man: So far, two trucks and a bus.

Bob: What do you get when you cross a parrot with a pig?
Rob: A loud bird that hogs the conversation.

Policeman: Your dog was seen chasing a family in a car.

Pet Owner: Don't be ridiculous. My dog doesn't even know how to drive.

Knock, knock.

Who's there?

Figs.

Figs who?

Figs the doorbell. It's broken!

Q: What's purple and conquers foreign lands?

A: Alexander the Grape.

Q: What do you call a huge herd of giraffes on the freeway?

A: A giraffic jam.

Customer: May I speak to the head boomerang salesman?

Receptionist: I'm sorry. Can he get back to you?

Did you hear about the guy who fell into an upholstery machine?

Don't worry. He's fully recovered now.

Bo: Hey, I heard you failed your karate test.
Asher: Yeah, I could kick myself.

A guy was observing two city workers in a park. One would dig a hole and the other would quickly fill it in. He finally asked what they were doing.

"Normally there are three of us. One guy plants the tree, but he's out sick today."

Patient: I'm always dizzy for a half hour when I get up in the morning. What should I do?
Doctor: Try getting up a half hour later.

Did you hear about the pancake chef who became an air traffic controller?

Now he's got planes stacked up all over the country.

I've got too many planes lined up! How waffle!

Piano Player: Do you think I have a gift for playing?

Listener: I don't know, but I'll give you one for stopping.

Q: Where do cows go on vacation?

A: To Cowlifornia.

Q: What do you call a guy who's hung on the wall?

A: Art.

I find that hard to believe.

Mom, everyone in town says I'm a liar!

Rocket Scientist: We are planning a rocket trip like no other. We are going to fly to the sun!

Reporter: That's ridiculous. You'll burn up as soon as you get near it!

Rocket Scientist: Ah ha! That's why we're going at night!

Navy Recruiter: Do you know how to swim?

Recruit: Why, aren't there enough ships?

Tongue Twisters

Give Papa a proper cup of coffee in a copper coffee cup.

Nat's knapsack strap snapped.

You know you need unique New York.

Bad money, mad bunny.

Stick strictly six stick stumps.

Ron: Are you going out with the librarian
Saturday night?

Don: No, she was already booked.

Diner: What's this fly doing in my ice cream?

Waiter: Probably cooling off. It gets pretty hot in
the soup.

Judge: Do you plead guilty or not guilty?

Convict: I don't know; I haven't heard the
evidence yet.

Customer: I'm looking for a new mattress.
Salesman: Do you want a spring mattress?
Customer: No thanks. I need one I can use all year.

Salesman: Would you like to buy a pocket calculator?
Customer: No thanks. I already know how many pockets I have.

Jon: I heard you got a job as a trash collector.
Ron: Yeah, I don't know much about it, but I figure I'll pick it up as I go along.

Teacher: Johnny, can you name the four seasons?
Johnny: Sure. Salt, pepper, vinegar, and mustard!

Teacher: Conner, how fast does light travel?
Conner: I don't know, but it gets here way too early in the morning.

Man at the Door: I'm here to tune your piano.
Piano Student: But I didn't send for you.
Man: No, but your neighbors did.

Manager: You can't help admiring our boss.
New Employee: Why is that?
Manager: 'Cause if you don't, you're fired.

Asher: I just rode the carousel 15 times.
Harper: Wow! You sure do get around, don't you?

Logan: This ointment makes my leg smart.
Rogan: Why don't you try rubbing it on your head?

Patient: Doctor, I can't seem to get to sleep at night.

Doctor: Well, lie on the edge of the bed, and soon you'll just drop right off.

Wow, the doctor was right!

Diner: Give me a spaghetti sandwich on rye.

Waiter: That's crazy! Nobody orders a spaghetti sandwich on rye!

Diner: You're right. Make it on whole wheat.

Police Captain: The thief got away, huh? Did you guard all the exits?

Patrolman: Yeah, we sure did, but he snuck out one of the entrances!

Bride: Darling, we've been married for 24 hours!

Groom: Yes, dear, it seems like only yesterday!

Jon: Why are you putting a bandage on your paycheck?

Ron: I just got a cut in my salary.

Mary: I'm going to take a milk bath.

Shari: Pasteurized?

Mary: No, just up to my shoulders.

Performer: Do you think my singing is becoming?

Audience Member: Yes, it's becoming annoying.

Two construction workers were having lunch outside their work site.

First Guy: Oh no, not again! A peanut butter sandwich! I can't stand it! Day in and day out, always a peanut butter sandwich! This is too much!!

Second Guy: Why don't you ask your wife to make you something different?

First Guy: I can't do that.

Second Guy: Why not?

First Guy: I make my own lunch!

Customer: I'd like a ticket to New York State, please.

Ticket Agent: Would you like to go by Buffalo?

Customer: No thanks. I'd rather take the bus.

Diner: This pea soup tastes like detergent!
Waiter: Oh, that must be the chicken soup. The
pea soup tastes like gasoline.

A scientist crossed poison ivy with a four-leaf clover and got a rash of good luck.

Mason: Do you have trouble making up your mind?
Jason: Well, yes and no.

Tim: Do you like your new job in the rubber band factory?

Jim: Oh, it's a snap.

Q: Who steals accessories off of cars and gives them to the poor?

A: Robin Hood Ornament.

Rick: A guy sold me the Nile River for $200.

Nick: Egypt you.

Doctor: You need glasses!
Patient: I already have glasses.
Doctor: Then *I* need glasses!

Remy: I'll give you $500 if you do the worrying for me.
Ava: Where's the $500?
Remy: That's your first worry.

Professor: I'm studying ancient history.
Teaching Assistant: Me too. Let's get together and talk about old times.

Captain: Sailor, did you clean the ship as ordered?

Sailor: Yes sir! I swabbed the deck, I cleaned the portholes, and I even swept the horizon with my telescope.

Don: I wish I had enough money to buy an elephant.

Ron: Why would you want an elephant?

Don: I don't. I just want the money.

Q: Why did the boy take his crayons to the zoo?

A: He wanted to try coloring outside the lions.

Diner: Is this peach or apple pie?
Waiter: Can't you tell by the taste?
Diner: No, I can't.
Waiter: Well then, what difference does it make?

Kid: A man came by to see you.
Mom: Did he have a bill?
Kid: No, just a regular nose.

Sir, there's a man outside
holding a drum.

Tell him to beat it.

Q: What's an astronaut's favorite food?

A: Launch meat!

Donny: Every night I take two 25-cent pieces to bed with me.

Lonny: What for?

Donny: They're my sleeping quarters.

Q: What does a lawyer wear to work?

A: A law suit.

Hannah: My new radio is so powerful that last night I got Mexico.

Deagan: So what? Last night I just opened my window and got Chile.

Did you hear about the guy who stole a truck filled with rubber bands?

He was put away for a long stretch.

Q: What do you call a chicken crossing the road?

A: Poultry in motion.

Ann: What do you get when you cross a maid with a giraffe?

Fran: I don't know, but my ceilings have never been cleaner!

Q: Why did the elephant stay home from the beach?

A: He couldn't find his trunks.

Q: What does the astronaut use to serve dinner?

A: A satellite dish.

Conner: Last night I slept on a 10-foot bed!

Chloe: That's a lot of bunk.

Q: How did the llama get to the movie premiere?

A: He went in a llamasine.

Q: Why did the stegosaurus need a bandage?

A: He had a dino-sore.

Q: Why did the forgetful lady go for a run?

A: She wanted to jog her memory.

Q: Why did the muffler quit the car business?

A: He was exhausted.

Knock, knock.

Who's there?

Classify.

Classify who?

Classify don't give you any homework, will you all pay attention?

Knock, knock.

Who's there?

Trainee.

Trainee who?

Trainee was trying to catch left 10 minutes ago.

Q: How do you write a note at the beach?

A: You use sandpaper.

Knock, knock.

Who's there?

Wafer.

Wafer who?

Wafer me. I'm almost ready.

Q: What do you call a deer in the car shouting directions?

A: A buck-seat driver.

Turn left here! No, no, the next street! Aren't you going a little fast? Slow down!

Q: Where do bees go on vacation?

A: Stingapore.

Knock, knock.
Who's there?
Apollo G.
Apollo G. who?
Apollo G. accepted.

Knock, knock.
Who's there?
Diploma.
Diploma who?
Diploma is here to fix da bathtub.

Knock, knock.
Who's there?
Huron.
Huron who?
Huron my foot. Ouch!

Knock, knock.
Who's there?
Tank.
Tank who?
You're welcome.

Knock, knock.
Who's there?
Dots.
Dots who?
Dots for me to know and you to find out.

Knock, knock.
Who's there?
Wire.
Wire who?
Wire you asking?

Q: What does a farmer give his wife for Valentine's Day?

A: Hogs and kisses.

Q: What does a French chef give his wife for Valentine's Day?

A: Hugs and quiches.

Q: What did one pickle say to the other?

A: "You mean a great dill to me."

A little girl was at her first wedding. She leaned over to her mom and whispered, "Why did the lady change her mind?"

"What do you mean, honey?"

"Well, she came down the aisle with one man and left with another."

Tongue Twister

Betty Botter bought some butter, but she said, "This butter's bitter. If I put it in my batter, it will make my batter bitter." So she bought a bit of butter, better than the bitter butter.

Man: Doctor, you've got to help me. I'm convinced I'm a doorbell.

Doctor: Well, take two aspirins and give me a ring in the morning.

Mike: What school do you have to drop out of to graduate from?

Ike: Parachute school!

Conner: Why did the boy take a ruler to bed?

Chloe: He wanted to see how long he slept.

Q: Where do eggs go on vacation?

A: New Yolk City.

Jon: Why was the guy fired from the automobile assembly line?

Ron: He was caught taking a brake.

Chad: What sits at the bottom of the ocean and shakes?

Rad: A nervous wreck.

Four out of three people have problems with fractions.

Harper: Why won't the mummy go on vacation?

Iris: He's afraid he might relax and unwind.

Yeah, looks like they broke in and stole everything but the soap, the shampoo, and the towels.

Those dirty crooks.

What did Delaware? A New Jersey.

Neighbor: Why are you wearing all those jackets while you're painting your house?

Fran: The paint can said to put on three coats.

Q: What do you get when you cross a cactus with a bicycle?

A: A flat tire.

Terry: Why are elephants so wrinkled?

Jerry: 'Cause they're almost impossible to iron.

Q: What is red, then yellow, then red, then yellow?

A: An apple that works part time as a banana.

Teacher: Tommy, can you use the word *aftermath* in a sentence?

Tommy: Sure. Aftermath class is over, I can go home.

Q: Why did the boy stay on the merry-go-round for three straight days?

A: He was trying to set a whirled record.

I stayed up all night wondering where the sun was. Then it dawned on me.

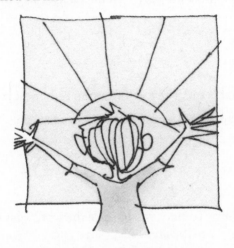

I bought a dictionary yesterday, but when I got home all the pages were blank. I don't have the words to describe how upset I am.

Q: Why do hens lay eggs?

A: 'Cause if they threw them, they'd break!

The forecast is clear and 60 degrees
with a 70% chance we're wrong.

Kylie: What does the horse say to the guy who lives next door?

Iris: "Hay, neeeiiggghhh-bor."

Q: How can you tell if there's an elephant in your bedroom?

A: By the big *E* on his pajamas.

Old Lady: Son, can you help me across the street?

Scout: Okay, but I can help you right here just as well.

Jo: Does February March?

Bo: Well, April May.

Q: What do dogs like to eat at the movies?

A: Pup-corn.

Stan: Did you hear the one about the three holes in the ground?

Dan: No, tell me.

Stan: Well, well, well.

Q: What kind of photos do turtles take?

A: Shellfies!

Guy in the Library: I'll have a cheeseburger and fries.

Librarian: Sir, you know this is a library.

Guy: Oh, sorry. (*Whispers*) I'll have a cheeseburger and fries.

Q: Who was the roundest knight at King Arthur's Round Table?

A: Sir Cumference.

Emily Biddle's Library of Book Titles:

Librarian Emily Biddle has a collection of unusual books in her bookmobile. Check out some of these titles:

1. *The Ball Game Will Go On* by Raynor Shine
2. *Use Those Credit Cards!* by Bill Melater
3. *Italian Cooking* by Liz Anya
4. *Join the Band!* by Clara Nett
5. *I'm So Stuffed* by Ada Lotte
6. *I Was Robbed* by Alma Money
7. *Where Are All the Cookies?* by Arthur Anymore
8. *Everything You Need to Know about Explosives* by Dinah Mite
9. *My Adventures in Space* by Andy Gravity

More Emily Biddle Book Titles:

Here are a few more interesting book titles from Emily's bookmobile:

1. *I'm Unemployed* by Anita Jobb
2. *Living with Robots* by Ann Droid
3. *Give Your Car a Tune-Up* by Carl Humm
4. *Where to Keep Your Plants* by Clay Potts
5. *Handling Dynamite* by E. Z. Duzzett
6. *Flips, Handstands, and Somersaults* by Jim Nastics
7. *How to Volunteer* by Linda Hand
8. *The Flooded Bathroom* by Lee King Fawcett
9. *Make Your Yard Look Great* by Moe D. Lawn
10. *Get Your Eyes Checked* by Seymour Clearly

Sandy Silverthorne, author of *Crack Yourself Up Jokes for Kids*, has been writing and illustrating books since 1988 and currently has over 600,000 copies in print. His award-winning Great Bible Adventure children's series with Harvest House sold over 170,000 copies and has been distributed in eight languages worldwide. He's written and illustrated over thirty books and has worked with such diverse clients as Universal Studios Tour, Doubleday Publishers, Penguin, World Vision, the University of Oregon, the Charlotte Hornets, and the Academy of Television Arts and Sciences. His recent series One-Minute Mysteries has already sold over 240,000 copies. Sandy has worked as a cartoonist, author, illustrator, actor, pastor, speaker, and comedian. Apparently it's hard for him to focus.

Connect with him at sandysilverthornebooks.com.